WHO DARE TO LIVE

THE MACMILLAN COMPANY
NEW YORK · BOSTON · CHICAGO · DALLAS
ATLANTA · SAN FRANCISCO

Who Dare To Live

BY

FREDERICK B. WATT
Lt.-Cmdr., R.C.N.V.R.

NEW YORK
THE MACMILLAN COMPANY

1943

DEDICATION

Two close shipmates are in this poem—though not as characters. The Irish enthusiasm of the first convinced me that its uncertain beginnings were worth seeing through. The second gave me no peace in the latter stages if I showed any signs of "slacking away" and so, on our last night together, the poem was complete and he was the first to hear it in its entirety, and suggested the title "Who Dare To Live".

To these two the book is dedicated:

LIEUTENANT **J. C. DWYER, R.C.N.V.R.**
(*Missing, September 26, 1942*)

COMMANDER **F. R. W. R. GOW, R.C.N.**
(*Missing, November 7, 1942*)

WHO DARE TO LIVE

Who Dare to Live

I HAVE loved ships too much, perhaps,
For my own good.
God help us sentimental chaps
When steel and wood
And faithful craftsmanship can so contrive
To work their spell,
Until that alchemy becomes alive
In you as well.

A brave man dies but once, I've heard,
And who am I
To doubt a poet's or a brave man's word?
We others try
To join the ragged band who share
The mortal pain
Of death repeated—yet who dare
To live again.

PART I

THERE was no longer any need to wait
Beside the postbox at the trelliced gate
Where, week on week, my anxious watch I'd kept;
But still I stayed while lazy raindrops crept
Down through my matted hair to streak my face.
"Sorry, dear Captain, but there is no place
For you at present. All our berths are filled—
Of late there's been more ships than Captains killed.
Added to that, it's really only fair
Younger, less tested men should do their share.
You, after all, are one of those who bore

1

All of the strain the first two years of war.
When there's an opening—" Oh, 'twas kind and slick,
But kinder had they said, "You've served your trick.
Face it, accept it. There can be no ship
For any man who once has lost his grip."

Nothing can strike more savagely than doubt
About a Master—once the word is out.
Cruel enough it were had it been true—
At forty-five a man should not be through;
But Dr. Warren's name was down to tell
The world that I was absolutely well;
Strong as a mule, those twenty pounds regained.
No trace of my strange weariness remained
But in its place the idle months had pent
A great, new vigour—urgent to be spent;
Something beyond ambition or the spell
That drives the seaman seaward, ill or well.

Numbly I brought to mind a scattered host
Of little birds off Massachusetts' coast.
Caught in migration, far from any lee,
A sudden gale had swept them out to sea.
On the chill day our vessel crossed their track
We saw the long, torn convoy beating back,
Rising and falling, harried here and there
By fitful currents in the troubled air.
Yet all the drive of tiny wings in flight
Was towards the land, too distant then for sight—
Checking with bearings man had yet to learn.
(We dipped our ensign as they crossed our stern.)

Courage and common purpose could not bring
An endless strength to battered heart and wing,
However, and the stragglers dropped in clouds

To claim the sanctuary of our shrouds.
Safety, to some, seemed more than they could stand;
They fluttered dead as they came down to land.
But others made their new position good
And twittered round the galley door or stood
Upon the deck, where men with sheepish grins
Offered them crumbs in old tobacco tins.

Up on the bridge we welcomed only one—
A yellow bit of fluff, completely done.
It struck the signal locker, where it lay
Caught in the cushioned folds of letter "J".
At first it seemed the little thing had died;
The Mate was set to chuck it overside
Until he felt a heart's quick, whispered beat,
And put it where the chartroom offered heat.
Then, as it came to life, the steward's lad
Produced an old canary cage we had.

Early next day I noted in the log
"Our guests are taking off despite the fog."
Drawn by a force too mighty to resist,
In swirling clouds they melted in the mist,
Spurning our safety for the distant land.
Even our prisoner stirred to the command.
Shrilling a constant protest from the cage,
He beat his wings against the bars in rage.
Lucky that bird, for it was mine to say
If it should have its chance; if it should stay—
No one, when my turn came, would understand
And spring the cage's door with friendly hand.

Stronger than fear of death, than love of ease,
Than all the brutal power of icy seas,
Stronger than hunger for a faithful wife,

I felt the stream that was my very life—
The stream of rusty hookers from the Tyne,
From Humber, Thames—the flowing battle line
That drew its strength from Belfast, Merseyside,
From Bristol Channel and the misty Clyde;
The stream that, were it dammed, meant England died.

I had scant cause to love it but its flood
Ran with a tide's insistence in my blood.
Terrible, England's need of that thin line
Of ships—but no less terrible was mine.

PART II

DEAR God, the steady, grinding ache
Of tautened nerves about to break!
Suddenly I was striding down
The gravelled road that led to town;
Walking like fury, deaf and blind,
Through the black storm that swept my mind.

How smooth the water where the ledge
Of roadway flanked the ocean's edge.
What soft, green peace!   A man could sleep
So dreamlessly ten fathoms deep.
Or could a coward rest—alone—
Where heroes were so richly sown?

Move on, you fool!   The pub's your spot—
Down there among the beery lot
Of bluff old sweats, grown soft too soon,
Who yarn away each afternoon.
You'll find warm friends 'midst smoky glow
Of wars won bravely—years ago.

4

A side-trail breasts the rugged hill
This side the town, by Baron's Mill;
Loops through thick walls of fir and pine
To almost reach the timber line.
Here I had seen, on one fine day,
Mount Baker, ninety miles away,

So close it seemed that I might speak
Across the Gulf and on the peak
My unraised voice would echo clear;
So close I saw the sunlight spear
With clean, straight shafts the crown of snow
Until it burned with lustrous glow.

Just what it did to me and why
I may not learn until I die.
I only know a feeling came
I never more would be the same;
That something new and pure and strong
Would stay with me my whole life long.

And so, today, by Baron's Mill,
I spurned the town and faced the hill,
Drawn as a hunter to a wood
Where once he'd found the shooting good,
Spurred as a tramp whom instinct sends
To some far port where once were friends.

Unbitter even when it flails
The Island during winter gales,
The Gulf of Georgia rain is kind;
It stirs the body, cleans the mind.
Today I knew its brisk caress
As part of May's pert loveliness—

Knew it with every upward stride
Upon the silent mountain side,
Until the song of lusty flesh
Wakened my heart to hope afresh,
Steadied my course till from the height
I faced the world with clearing sight.

If from the Gulf the veil of gray
Had suddenly been whipped away,
And brought Mount Baker to my eyes
I would have known a scant surprise,
For through the swirl of rain-filled air
I somehow felt it shining there.

Yet all that really met my gaze
Was dun sea blending with the haze
Along the shore and steep below,
The little world I'd come to know—
The world that once had been the prize
I'd sought this side of Paradise.

Show me the salt who's known the smile
Of beautiful Vancouver's Isle,
And I will promise you a man
Whose life is governed by a plan.
Years are but stepping-stones to reach
The day he settles on the beach.

So 'twas with me since that first time
I'd seen the purple mountains climb
Out of the quiet sea that waits
Inside the Juan de Fuca Straits.
Here clung my dream as years drove past—
And now the dream was real at last.

Slowly I followed every line
Of Fairlee's eastern stand of pine,
Its apple orchard, bursting white,
The winding trout stream to the right,
The kitchen garden, and the pen
Where Bessie knew each strutting hen.

Among the oaks the gabled roof
Flaunted its crimson as a proof
That here lived folk who used their paint
Without a mortgage's restraint—
And down the shrub-walled path the gate
Which I had opened—just too late.

*   *   *

August of Nineteen Thirty-Nine!
That was the month I was to sign
The papers that made Fairlee mine.

And Bess had urged me go ahead.
"Even if this means war," she said,
"It's got to end some time and then
We'll have our chance to start again.
Let it be waiting.   Let it be
Our one fixed light of certainty."

But I had answered, "Time enough
When Hitler has run out his bluff.
I want no heaven to regret
Should all this brew of hell upset."
I thought if I was hard and curt
She wouldn't know how much it hurt.

Signed for a final, six months' trip
I was in Biscay on my ship
When Hitler proved, with Danzig's fall,
He was in earnest after all.
It was a long year later when
We two spoke Fairlee's name again.

PART III

WAR, I suppose, comes pretty sharp and shaking
To one whose peacetime calling hugs the shore.
All that was certain goes in one swift breaking
Of that safe world on which he set his store.
Even the soldier, trained to match the hour,
Knows a dramatic shock which ends his play,
Bringing its sudden sense of timely power—
Only with seamen old sensations stay.

Kissing my Bessie on the night of sailing
There was no panicked clinging of our lips
Even though war was near—no futile railing—
Parting is life to those whose lives are ships.
Peacetime or wartime, there the sea was waiting,
Bearing the sound ships, burying the lame,
Scornful of human loving, human hating—
Colder than death, more vital than a flame.

Little was changed when Sparks, quite unexcited,
Stumped through the wheelhouse door and said, "It's come."
There was scant heat to fires that message lighted,
There was scant pain to nerves already numb.
Just for a moment Bessie, back in Devon,
Faced me with stricken eyes and features gray—
Hell had tipped over, even into heaven
Waiting at Fairlee, half the world away.

8

Then she was gone and there were things for doing
Swiftly, as we'd been warned before we sailed.
Orders were opened—words that set us slewing
Off on another track as morning paled.
Into the rising swells our hawses bunted,
Swells that were running now with hidden hate
Seeping from hidden men—and we, the hunted,
Shrugged and accepted there our new estate.

Nothing more great to do than just maintaining
The simple trade by which we earned our bread;
Nothing complex that needed glib explaining—
Our course was plotted, speed was "Full ahead".
And yet there couldn't be complete ignoring
Of something, deep inside, which stirred and warmed—
Knowledge that there would never be restoring
Of battlements we held, were once they stormed.

At least, I felt it.   There could be no saying
If Bos'n, as he checked the lifeboat gear,
Gave it a thought at all.   Beneath the graying
Great shock of hair his weathered face was clear,
Nothing revealed except where wind and ocean
Had drawn it strangely patient, deeply wise.
Only the sea, it seemed, had his devotion—
The sea which gave the colour to his eyes.

What of the others?   Could I speak for Harrow,
The messboy who was barely turned fifteen,
Dancing on deck, as feckless as a sparrow,
His snub nose and his language none too clean?
Or Cole, the Mate, who seldom ceased his pacing
While standing watch—had he a greater care
Than that which he admitted he was facing—
The child his ailing wife was soon to bear?

9

What was the difference?   Bess had once persisted,
"If thoughts start singing in you, let them sing.
They're to be trusted, darling, not resisted,
As long as they've a decent, honest ring."
And if strange music, fitful and unbidden
Should reach my ears as England's path lay grim,
Surely there must be other listeners hidden
In quiet Bos'n and the likes of him.

Surely they heard it, too, and surely heeded
The long-returning voice that, sudden, said
Inside a man, "See here, you're really needed,
And no one other chap will do instead."
Surely it cut the stench of Harrow's galley,
Where youth claimed manhood through a dirty quip,
And, in his darkened cabin off the alley,
Found fumbling Cole—and gave him back his grip.

During the weeks that followed I grew certain
About it all.   I'd sense it when I saw
Our convoy hold formation as a curtain
Of fog bore down, though every human law
Of selfish preservation shouted, "Scatter!
Find sea-room for yourself!"   Aye, bit by bit
Out of the stuff soft years had left a-tatter
A rough and honest fabric was being knit.

Vessels in convoy spared themselves excuses
When failure came.   Their reasoning was stark
Because a clever tongue, with all its uses,
Would not divert torpedoes in the dark;
And there was little point in smooth explaining
Of funnel smoke belched, careless, 'gainst the sky
And seen for miles—if there was nought remaining
But wreckage where the watchful foe stood by.

All of the slag thrown up in peacetime brawling
For trade was smelted down to common trust,
By men brought back to precepts of their calling
Through no fine choice, but simply since they must.
Willing, unwilling, each was soon to master
The lesson men ashore had yet to learn—
That danger lay ahead, but swift disaster
Awaited stragglers, saving fuel astern.

PART IV

RARELY, with no sound explanation,
The shipping world beholds creation
Of one strange vessel which bewilders
The very men who were her builders.
Sister, perhaps, of some sea-slattern
With whom she's shared a common pattern,
She brings, unasked, a stirring measure
Of virtue.   Mine was such a treasure.

As though he'd known I had intended
To quit him when the voyage ended,
Owner had offered, richly laden,
The newest freighter—on her maiden.
If ever craft had power of shaking
The shoreward course I'd planned on taking,
It was *Bergetta*; from first meeting
She'd set my seaman's pulses beating.

Fresh from her trials I found her waiting,
Without a scratch upon her plating.
Innocent yet of wind and weather,
The smells of paint and brand-new leather
Hung in her cabins.   Yet already

I felt her breathing, quiet, steady.
Ships, to have souls, must mostly win them;
A few are born with spirit in them.

Such was *Bergetta*; all the staring
Of boats whose basin she was sharing
Left her unmoved. She sat the water
As sure, as poised as Neptune's daughter,
Beneath their gray, hard-bitten searching.
What if she'd yet to taste the lurching
Of Western Ocean, grimly feathered?
She could take anything *they'd* weathered!

Nothing that happened ever altered
My estimate. She never faltered
In all the time I was to know her.
Cross-swells could wrack her, head winds slow her
But never once, though seas were hulking,
Was man to catch *Bergetta* sulking;
Honest, courageous—bluff bow tossing
To every threat of every crossing.

Strength of her Diesels, smoothly coursing,
Gave her thirteen—and then not forcing.
(Twelve had been asked of her designer.)
The engines of a gaudy liner
Were not more spotless, smartly tended,
As through her skylights there ascended
The warm, exciting breath of power,
With lube and fuel oil sweetly sour.

Berthed at her dock she was as willing
As when her scuppers had been spilling.
Sure to the touch, her deck-gear limber
Could hoist a truck or baulk of timber
With equal ease—and deftly stow it.

"Speed is the watchword and we know it,"
Her winches sang—and to their singing
Six thousand tons were inboard swinging.

No sullen slave to man who made her—
For all that he might sell or trade her—
She gave, with that free joy of giving,
The faithfulness of something living—
Living and incorrupt.   No wonder
Whene'er I saw some ship go under
My breath, stabbed sharp with fear, came faster;
Fear for *Bergetta*—not her Master.

PART V

WE THOUGHT it bad enough that first, long winter,
What with the subs and new magnetic mines.
For us the war was savage, in the open,
No sheltering Maginot or Siegfried lines
Unless you counted those the Navies built us,
British and French, wherever convoys sailed—
Walls that, when things went well, you took for granted
And cursed with bitter humour when they failed.

So, while the Air Force dribbled gentle leaflets
On Germany, and growling armies warred
To keep the martial flame alive with concerts
And other antidotes for getting bored,
Death limbered up in earnest on the Western
And where the North Sea chop slashed salty cold;
We thought it bad enough that first, long winter
When terse, grim yarns in wharfside pubs were told.

Yarns about ships we knew.   I still remember
How hard I took the sinking of a boat,

Those early days; how startled to discover
That scores of others still remained afloat.
Somehow, when someone went who'd been familiar,
It seemed the whole, wide ocean should be bare;
That all the world you'd known was doomed and writhing
Within a single blazing tanker's glare.

Such as when Sampson went—old Barney Sampson
With whom I'd served my first apprenticeship
Near thirty years before; great, gusty Barney
Who held existence in his easy grip
Like some amusing curio he'd purchased
Lightly, yet as he aged, had grown to love;
Who barged, hell-roaring, into your affections
Against your will—yet never seemed to shove.

There were few ports I'd known that had no memory
Of Captain Sampson. West or south or east
He was forever topping some horizon
At times when you expected him the least.
Broad as the sea, as wild, as grimly faithful,
As endlessly alive—his creaming wake
Had brought sound satisfaction to his owners,
Yet would have pleased a Frobisher or Drake.

Strangely, Bess liked him; how we laughed together
When last the three of us, on Merseyside,
Stepped out to flicks and supper on the evening
Before the westbound convoy caught the tide.
Bess had come up from Plymouth to be with me
For those swift days allowed us to discharge;
Tired and subdued she'd seemed till we encountered
The tanker, *Bream*, with Barney bulking large.

Just as some least-expected person offers
The rock on which a marriage runs aground,

Some other, even stranger, brings a moment
In which new freedom suddenly is found.
That was what Barney did for me and Bessie
When precious hours, melting, left us tense.
Somehow his booming laughter made for quiet
And somehow all his nonsense made for sense.

Later, at Halifax, bound eastward, loaded,
I saw him once again—a grizzled Jove
Who held a restaurant rapt as he made havoc
Of two huge lobsters, fresh from Peggy's Cove.
One of them would have stuffed an average mortal
Until he gagged, but Barney in his stride
Had ten men's appetite for life and living—
Nor was the going modest when he died.

That came just ten days later— in the Twenties—
With sea and sky fused formlessly at dawn.
Bream lay inside *Bergetta*, just to starboard,
A smudged, dark shape some youngster might have drawn.
And suddenly it happened, I was looking
In her direction when there came the flash.
"Good Christ! She's filled with aviation spirit!"
A voice cried out. I never heard the crash;

I only saw *Bream's* slender foremast leaping
Uprooted from the deck—and then the light
Was gone. For ten sick heartbeats we were blinded,
But slowly there appeared to tortured sight
A black and mighty shadow—rising, rising
In solid mass to smother feeble day—
A ghastly, greasy mushroom swelling skyward—
And locked within its heart the tanker lay.

Upward and upward fought the sable giant,
Entrapped and mad and straining to be free,

'Till, with a roar, the very dawn exploded
And all the world was flaming sky and sea.
An hour later everything was over—
The *Bream* was gone, the sky was clean astern,
But sight and smell still lived the dreadful minutes.
It isn't nice to watch a shipmate burn.

And still I heard his ready laughter rising
Above the blazing cargo's thundered note,
And crazy words, "I'll match my Viking's funeral
With that of any Admiral afloat!"
But on towards afternoon my ears stopped ringing,
The biting stench inside my nostrils cleared,
And all was as it should be—save the ocean
Which stretched like burned-off prairie, sullen, seared.

We thought it bad enough, that first long winter
When ships were hunted down in ones and twos.
It seemed a heavy price that we were paying
To keep alive a war we couldn't lose.
Impatiently we waited spring, when armies
Of reawakened France should cross the Rhine
To quickly end it all, to bring back reason,
To speed the day when Fairlee should be mine.

PART VI

Broadway, ablaze and roaring, failed to warm
The chill about my heart, nor could the storm
Of pleasure-sated thousands wash away
The feel of Dunkirk's beaches and the gray
Of Channel mists.   Aboard the Brooklyn train
The sledge of panic hammered at my brain
And raised few sparks of courage, for it struck
On faith with the consistency of muck.

Aboard *Bergetta*, patient at her pier,
I paused beside the Bos'n's port to hear
The tireless, hard-boiled radio repeat,
"British bombard their former Ally's fleet."
"Choke it!" there came the Donkeyman's command.
"There's just so much a decent bloke can stand."
The broadcast snapped. I heard the Bos'n tell
His mates, "There will be joy tonight in hell."

Another muttered, "Where's it all to end?
Who is to stop this turning friend on friend?"
The Bos'n's laugh was soft as it was rare.
"Fellows like you," he said, "and such as care
To stick it out." The other man was slow
To answer; then, at last, he spat, "That's so.
Who but the likes of me, who cannot choose?"
"I know a Pole," said Bos', "who'd fill your shoes

"And thank his God." The slapping of the tide
And muffled noises on Manhattan side
Broke loudly as a sudden quiet claimed
Bergetta and her men. There was no shamed
Denial by the chap, no further word—
And finally a door slammed and I heard
Him clumping for'ard. Then the Bos'n's voice,
"The ruddy fool *believes* he has no choice!"

"And *has* he?" pressed the Donkeyman. "Have you?"
Countered the Bos'n. "Never thought it through,"
Dodged Donkeyman. "I only know I'm scared
As any rabbit's son. I've been prepared
To face the worst since ever France went flat,
But, damn it, this is even worse than that.
What, with one Navy, will the convoys do?
God knows we've caught it stiff enough with two."

Bos'n found lazy interest in his pipe.
He tapped and scraped it till the time was ripe
To speak again. "If Churchill came tonight
And said, 'Well, lads, we've picked a losing fight.'
What, should he offer, would you have him do?"
The other jibed, "I'd shove him on to you
To learn the answers that you never give.
I know them—sure—but, hell, I want to live!"

Bos' spoke three words, and no hydraulic ram
Could have hit harder—"So did Rotterdam."

"All right, all right," said Donkeyman. "I seem
To get exactly nowhere, blowing steam.
Mine are the kind who'd sooner take a drink
To help unsnarl a mess—than stop to think."
"Who wouldn't?" asked the Bos'n. "Men like you
And Skipper," snapped the Donkeyman. "A few
Who grab that thing called duty, since you choose
To live your lives with nothing else to lose."

Bos' thought that over. "Have you seen, at all,
The lass who hangs upon the Old Man's wall?"
"Better than that," said Donkeyman, "I've seen
Her come aboard at Liverpool—the queen."
"Think you," urged Bos', "a man would gladly clutch
At duty if that woman loved him much?"
"There are some things I've never understood,"
The other said. "But, yes—I think he would."

Caught in the silence, I became aware
Of what a fool I'd be found snooping there.
Swiftly I tiptoed down the deck and clung
To furtive paths with deepest shadows hung
Until, up topsides, where I lived alone,

The bulwark of my day-room door was thrown
Against the world—the world that must not know
The loneliness that Masters undergo.

Here you could sense a woman's thoughtful hand—
Some bits of chintz, a well-braced flower-stand
Whose soft-exploding fern held, clean and fair,
The touch of fingers that had put it there.
Above my desk a single light gave life
To that fine face. When strangers asked, "Your wife?"
Their suddenly excited tones inferred,
"Good Lord! Imagine! Married to this bird!"

Who was to blame them? Reason had not been
A factor when we married in 'Nineteen.
Impulse, alone, had guided Bess to choose
A freighter, on a Caribbean cruise,
In which to flee the crazy life that thrived
Where fragments of her shattered world survived.
Sick of amusements quick to flame and die,
She'd cast for something new—and there was I.

Findlay, the Master, cynical and tight,
Congratulated us with grim delight,
Asking, "Just tell me, ma'm, how do you rate
A catch like this—my blasted Second Mate?
What can you offer?" Bess had caught my arm
Before I did the smirking rumpot harm,
Laughing, "Ah, Captain, set your fears at rest.
Whatever I've to give will be my best."

Now, in my cabin, underneath her eyes
That smiled, yet were so steady and so wise,
I knew, as I had known through hell and heaven,
Hers was no thoughtless promise gaily given.

Many the times her failure would have pleased
The rebel in me, for it would have eased
The unrelenting rightness of her claim
To every decent instinct in my frame.

Bos'n had asked, "D'you think a man would clutch
At duty if that woman loved him much?"
And Donkeyman, who really understood,
Had known the answer: "Yes, I think he would."

PART VII

PERHAPS beyond the inner gates
Some special seamen's heaven waits
For those strange souls, unsaved, unblessed,
Who will not or who cannot rest;
A haven built for recompense
To mortal lives that made no sense.

For surely there is little sane
In men who worship, heart and brain,
An all-demanding mistress—still
Make constant quarrel with her will;
Who ride her winds like reckless gods,
Yet dream the dreams of landward clods.

In any setting but the sea
There would have been no Bess for me.
An orphan out of Devonport
Stood well to leeward of her sort—
A Colonel's daughter, and a girl
Whose Aunt was married to an Earl.

But cargo boats that only go
A dozen passengers or so
Are little isles of love and hate,

On which a hawse-pipe Second Mate
May even play a daring hand
In quarters where he knows command.

A uniform of spotless whites
Is kingly stuff on tropic nights,
And there is power in the feel
Of every swell beneath the keel.

Before the voyage half was done
My Bessie and the sea were one,
A blended current, fit to shake
A lad like me from truck to strake.

Bess had three hundred pounds a year
And I—I scarcely owned my gear.
But in the magic of those days
It never was a point to raise.
Ah youth, when even logic fails
To dull the sheen of fairy tales!

No fairy tale could quite transcend
A certain fact at journey's end,
However.   Bess's plan to ship
As stewardess the coming trip
Met opposition, simply stated:
"The state of marriage was created—"
And whether we concurred or no,
The fact undoubtedly was so.

So when I sailed, I sailed alone,
And any pain I'd ever known
Was but a twinge to that which ripped
My very innards as we slipped.
No man less grateful ever stood
In imminence of fatherhood.

At times I didn't even dare
To picture Bessie stranded there
Among her relatives, who made
Terse reference to our "escapade",
But slowly fight within me slacked.
I saw how hopeless was our pact;

I saw it was no use to bluff
(Self-pity is dramatic stuff);
That there had never been a hope
For fragile human love to cope
With class-forged barbed wire, line on line,
That ranged between her world and mine.

Yet when, months later, I returned
My proffered martyrdom was spurned
With quiet laughter.   Bess had grown
So different in those days alone.
Of frightened girl there was no trace;
A lovely woman filled her place.

"What, give you up?" she scoffed, arms tight
About me in the pulsing night.
"Give up my only chance to feel
I have a part in something real!
Ah no, my darling, come what may,
This sailor's woman must I stay."

Night's velvet had been trimmed with gold
Before her tale was simply told;
Of frantic weeks, of lone suspense,
Of friends who cried, "Use common sense.
Hell travels with that type of man,
Get out from under while you can."

"And being what I was," she said,
"I very nearly wished you dead,

Until one night in my despair
I somehow felt my father there—
He died when he was thirty-nine
With Allenby in Palestine.

"Ah, how I loved him!   How I cried
Against his God, the day he died,
The God he claimed had been so near
At night when desert skies were clear,
That he heard Him speak; his Lord
Who gave him dreams, yet as they soared
Stood, passive by, until they fell
Before a Turkish shrapnel shell.

"My bitterness was quick excuse
To play the leavings fast and loose
Until *you* came—and even you
Went on, and none would see me through
The frightful days, except to nurse
My selfish fear—and make it worse—

"Then, then, thank God, my memory went
To one last letter Dad had sent:

" 'Sweet Bess—I hope I have been true
To two great passions—England, you—
As soldiers measure faithfulness.
I've loved my Maker rather less,
But now, through clearer eyes, I see
I cannot separate the three.

" 'If God's own Son could face with hope
His zero hour from this slope
Where we are camped—this bleakest hill—
Then even I may yet fulfill
Some sense of having lived for more
Than victory in a passing war.

" 'For all of England that is fair
Is what our dear Lord planted there;
And all of England that is ill
Is where we've forced our pagan will;
And all of England that shall be
Grows fine or false in men like me.

" 'So, Sweet, tonight has come a start
Of reborn England in my heart,
And nothing I shall do must blur
Those things I covet most for her—
Those clean, tough qualities that He
Gave fishermen in Galilee.'

"As I remembered," Bess went on,
"Confusion suddenly was gone
And quietly I understood
What Dad had known—and it was good
To be alone, as he had been,
With dreams of England, tough and clean.

"In silence of my heart I knew
Exactly what I had to do.
And it is done; whatever life
Holds out from now, I am your wife—
Your home is mine, and it shall stand,
An outpost of that better land.

"No bands, no flags, no cash to burn
(We're going to live on what you earn
Until our child is twenty-one),
But love and selflessness and fun!
Who knows, you'll make me uncrowned queen
Of England's Mercantile Marine!

"And men will come to us and say,
'This was the home which showed the way
To honest clearing of disputes,
Distrust cut cleanly at the roots—'
Here, as your wife, I stake my claim
To freedom worthy of the name."

Poor Bess! She couldn't see, as I,
That freedom's price came grimly high
For merchant seamen—and the road
Was long, and hunger was the goad,
Not England, when Depression came—
Yet how she stuck it just the same!

Aye, when I shipped before the mast
To dodge the dole, she still held fast
To her agreement; when the numb
Despair of living in a slum
Was mine, she only said, "We've found
A really honest battleground."

So she remained until the turn
Of trade, where I at last could earn
A Master's place, a Master's pay.
And then there came the magic day
When lovely Fairlee hove in sight,
To burn a constant beacon light.

Fairlee—not just a plot of land,
But time and means to understand
So many things, brushed swift aside
For twenty years to catch a tide;
To join a ship, to seek a berth,
To chase a living 'round the earth—
So many things that could not wait
Much longer in unsettled state.

PART VIII

SILENT, the lifeboat rose and fell
In utter loneliness that tripped
Your heart a beat.   The Gulf Stream swell
Claimed yet ignored it as it slipped
From crest to crest—a slug-like thing
Upon an ocean's skin that crawled
With horror.   It was early spring—
And on the thwarts the dead were sprawled.

Out on the far Pacific slope
The dogwood blossom's fragile breath
Was fresh on Fairlee, fresh with hope,
But here the spring brought only death;
The same grim fruit of early fall;
The same harsh crop by winter sown—
Old Donkeyman had seen it all;
What could one Navy do alone?

What it could do was done.   No flesh
Or steel had ever met such strain
And held together.   Vessels fresh
From drydock, men of rested brain
Might well have flinched—but here were craft
With rivets gone and plates a-rust,
Pounded and weary fore and aft
Yet held, unceasing, to their trust.

Men to whom port was home no more
But only somewhere to abide,
A nightmare pause to swift restore
The bunkers trim 'twixt tide and tide.
Then to the fight again—to bluff
The world that nothing much was wrong,

That one destroyer was enough
To guard a convoy fifty strong;

That one tired, faithful watchdog's teeth
Could turn the wolf-pack as it slashed
Abeam, astern, above, beneath!
No wonder when the German smashed
Full-fury, that the losses soared—
Yet those who dawdled to discuss
"What price the Navy?"—those who scored
Its failure were not chaps like us.

Not us who witnessed, day on day,
The march of hearts that would not break,
The hearts that beat on *Jervis Bay*
And pulsed in each destroyer's wake.
The miracle was that they tried
Against such odds; yet in the face
Of all they did the freighters died
Too fast for shipyards to replace.

All through the winter months we knew
The certainty that left you sick—
That two from four left only two
In any man's arithmetic;
And even if you added one
The final answer still was plain:
Each grim, succeeding question done
Reduced the principal again.

These were not figures in a book
But figures in your soul that ate
Like acid.   You had just to look
At each new convoy, and the weight
Of doubt was like a sodden coat

Upon your back.   You knew the war
Ran strong against you—marked each boat—
And few there were you'd known before.

Here was a Dutchman, freeboard low,
And superstructure open wide
To catch the cooling winds that blow
Where Sourabaya traders ride.
Here a Norwegian, stanchions bare
Where awnings once had shed the sun
That blesses lucky men who share
The Rio de la Plata run.

This was no place for such as they;
The tropic paint still on their flanks,
Their heatless shelters caked with spray
That strikes, half-solid, on the Banks.
This was no place for native crews,
Curled up and numb like frozen bees—
But when you fight for life you use
Just what you have, not what you please.

And if the North Atlantic fleet
Of sturdy tramps was harried thin
There only was one means to meet
The deficit.   We still could win
If somehow we could hold the length
Of sea that kept the Island fed,
Till summer brought new escort strength
And fresh-built tonnage forged ahead.

So, without break, the convoys stood
To seaward on their 'periled track,
Running the gauntlet where they could.
Atlantic flung their wreckage back

When luck was out.   Such wreckage rode
The Gulf Stream on this day in spring—
A lifeboat with a dismal load,
Its mainsail like a broken wing.

There, 'mid the nerveless limbs, outflung,
And drawn, dead faces, one we found
Who still was breathing.   He was young
As Masters went.   His hand was 'round
The tiller still and he was braced
Commandingly, although his eyes
Were caverns in a scrubby waste
From which no glint of sense would rise.

Quickly his men were searched and sunk
(How gratefully they slipped to rest!),
And, barely conscious, in my bunk
We stowed the unexpected guest,
While Cole, the Mate, with sudden mirth
Born in the hell of endless strain,
Giggled, "I scarcely think he's worth
The trouble, sir, to entertain."

PART IX

THE steward threw the starboard deadlight wide
And sunlight tumbled in.   The golden stream
Revealed the lone survivor, open-eyed,
And, like a spotlight, held him in its gleam.
I moved to black it out again but he
Halted me with the thinnest sort of smile.
"The sun and I are friends, so let it be.
I've had enough of darkness for a while."

"Two solid days and nights of it," I said,
"But now you're going to be as right as rain."
His blonde hair made a halo 'bout his head
And that which marked his face was more than pain.
He held his hands up, hands I'd had to dress,
With every finger blackened by gangrene.
"The surgeons won't leave much of these, I guess?"
And I, I didn't answer—for I'd seen.

How I recall him lying in the light
That set the stubble of his beard aglow!
"If you were me," he questioned, "would you fight
Or would you take a chance like this and go?"
I didn't have to ask him what he meant
(Exposure often takes its time to kill),
For whether this Norwegian stayed or went
Hung balanced on a single act of will.

"Life's sweet," I told him.   "So," he said, "was she
I left behind in Bergen; so were they
Who called me father; so was Norway—free.
Already half my life is cut away
And what remains is practice for the knife.
Why struggle?" "I'm no person to reply
To that," I said, "but if you met my wife
She'd claim that something more than you would die."

The flicker of a smile came slowly—passed.
"But what do you think?   You've a mind as well."
"I often question that," I said at last.
"I've only instinct, and it's mixed as hell.
If I were in your place I'd likely quit—
Being me—and yet a fellow never knows—
My wife would say—"   Again he smiled a bit
And sighed, and then I saw his eyelids close.

"He's gone," I thought, and felt a sudden draught
Of fear.   This Master Mariner contained
The concentrated spirit of a craft
And all her crew; that life, while it remained,
Was still a fighting promise.   I suppose
I was the least unnerved, but as I stood
And held my breath, it hit me, "If he goes
Then freedom goes—and Fairlee goes—for good—"

Yet, as I scrutinized the face at peace,
The truth came, driving strong, through my concern.
No resignation brought him that release
But firm decision.   I'd seen Bos'n turn
With such a look to undertake some task
Upon the boiling foredeck, tempest-blown—
Some tricky job he'd never think to ask
The watch to do, yet which he did alone.

So Peter Dalsbo lived.   'Till we made port
My cabin ceased to be a hermit's cave,
And every hour there was all too short
To hoard the rich companionship he gave.
In that brief week I opened up my mind
As I had never done with any man,
And answers I had never hoped to find
Took form while life assumed a clearer plan.

It wasn't what he said; it was the way
That he accepted facts and shaped his course,
Convinced that he had still a part to play.
No loss of ship, of crew, of home, could force
His quiet spirit down when once he gave
His undramatic promise to go on.
It wasn't just a case of being brave—
What he possessed was bigger—and it shone.

He seldom talked about the war; he spoke
Of winter's sun against the mountain snow
In Bergensfjord; of how the morning broke
Its arrows on the shield of sea below.
He told me of the tiny valley farm
(A hundred years his salty clan's retreat)
Which dangled every voyage like a charm
Upon a chain of days when life was sweet.

At times he called his children to my room.
They filled the place with voices and the faint,
Exciting atmosphere of fresh-burst bloom.
Of crippled hands I never heard complaint
Once reach his lips.   He simply touched the past
Where it was good and brought it up to date
With confidence that decent things would last
If fought for—and he fought—but not with hate.

Here was a man of Barney Sampson's mould
In some respects.   He had the same fine zest
For all the ocean's pageant and the cold
Hard logic of her ways.   He, too, could jest
At all her moods, no matter what they cost—
But softly, free of any human pride.
He held what Barney played with 'till he lost;
He understood, where Barney just defied.

I told him that he left me greatly shamed—
I, who possessed so much yet felt betrayed
By dreams denied.   He laughingly disclaimed
The right to judge.   "Each fellow to his trade
And sailoring is mine, by choice and birth.
I've learned no other—and it's honest bread.
I know that when I give it all I'm worth
The voyage pays, whatever lies ahead."

If only we had had a month to spend
Together, not a swiftly slipping week,
I might have found myself—not just a friend;
I even might have learned, in time, to speak
My doubts instead of nursing them.   Too soon
We saw Manhattan's shining towers soar
Through silver mist one April afternoon.
That night he was in hospital ashore.

Before he left he said, "I won't forget
The faith that touched your voice, that lit your eye,
The morning that you put me in your debt—
The morning I decided not to die."
"Belay," I growled.   "I simply said, 'My wife—' "
"Exactly," he returned, "but, just the same,
That's how faith runs.   It leaps from life to life
Until, one day, you find from whence it came."

PART X

THAT was a record homeward trip.
We went straight through without a loss,
The weather perfect right across,
And there was music in the ship—

The same deep music I had heard
In early war days; and the sea
Respun her youthful charm for me.
Forgotten urges warmed and stirred.

Bergetta berthed by Mersey's shore.
I wired to Bessie, "Let's slip down
And spend a week of leave in Town—"
(The first I'd taken since the war.)

At Euston Station when we met
She eyed me anxiously—then smiled,
As frankly happy as a child
Who'd won a little, secret bet.

She laughed. "The man has lost his wits.
Dog-tired from perils of the deep
And looking for a place to sleep,
He picks on London in the blitz."

"Where else could you and I have fun?"
I countered. "There are still some shows—"
"Of course," said Bess, "and then—who knows—
You might find time to see your son."

"D'you mind?" I asked. She dropped the jest
And answered low, "Of all the ways
We could have spent these precious days,
Oh darling, this is quite the best."

We found some digs near Derek's 'drome
And, thrice that week, between the flights
That took him up aloft at nights,
He managed several hours "at home".

Fruitful this seed that I had sown—
A fighter pilot, hard and lean,
A grave-eyed stranger who had been
The little boy I'd scarcely known.

Because in later years I'd learned
To close my mind when yearning pained,
Blurred memories of the lad remained—
But now, clean-edged, they all returned;

Clean-edged and oh, so sharply sweet!—
A small face pressed against a pane,
A laugh as fresh as April rain,
And wee legs twinkling down a street.

So poised he was (and I so shy),
So much like Bess, and yet a man!
Emotion rose in me and ran
From wells I had believed were dry.

It never struck me to resent
The shortness of this great reprieve,
That every time he had to leave
It was to tortured skies he went,

Nor that my time with Bess was tuned
To nights that shook with cordite's thud,
And low-hung clouds were dipped in blood
As London took another wound.

The night before I had to go
The very firmament was fired.
Next morning Derek's eyes were tired
But nothing dulled his "Cheerio!"

The quiet firmness of his grip!
No taut "Goodbye", but in that hand
I felt each youngster of his band
Accepting me in fellowship.

Nine-tenths of him was Bess, for sure—
God knew, I'd played a scruffy part—
Yet, chances were, that in his heart
Some spark I'd struck might yet endure,

Some magic drawn from sea-born things
To pass to comrades of the height—
"The few", who in their falcon flight,
Bore all of England on their wings.

PART XI

THREE days out the blow came down
On our westward-floating town;
First with shrapnel-bursts of rain
Ripping through each well-kept lane,
Then with great, explosive swells,
Ponderous as twelve-inch shells.
Hard upon the beam they struck,
Spurting to the foremast truck,
'Till the ships in ballast swung
With their bells all giving tongue.
In the onslaught of the storm
Streets of vessels lost their form—
Scattered in the driving gloom
While the outer lines made room,
Then, at dusk—the weather worse—
Came the order to disperse.

Four wild days and nights it blew.
On the second we hove to—
Careless of our forward drive,
Quite content to stay alive.
There were times the broken sea
Filled the space where sky should be
As *Bergetta*, plunging light,
Shuddered like a horse afright.
Yet, with combers boarding green,

This was fighting fair and clean.
Through the strain, the sleep denied,
Something glowed and satisfied.

Finally the tempest's shout
Died away.   The stars came out
And a timid moon.   The glow
Dusted swells that, row on row,
Stretched like empty opera stalls
When the fireproof curtain falls
And the glooming house is filled
With the ghosts of trumpets stilled.

Not a mast or wisp of smoke
Met our eyes when morning broke,
But a sight we took at noon
Promised us some comfort soon.
"Nineteen-Twenty-West" it read
And the Commodore had said,
"Submarines don't seem to thrive
Farther west than Twenty-Five.
Mind the early Twenties, though—
Not a place to loaf, you know."

One day more should see us clear
Of that lonely fringe of fear
And *Bergetta* seemed to sense
How things stood.   There was a tense
Urgency behind the song
Of her engines and her strong
Shouldering of every swell.

Then we heard the lookout yell,
"Plane to port!"   Snapped Cole, "Who cares?
Tell us if it's ours or theirs!"
Drifting down the sun she came,

Almost hidden in its flame,
And her deep-toned motors told
She was big.   The thunder rolled
Louder, louder—while the bong
Of *Bergetta's* "Action" gong
Brought the guns' crews tumbling out.
Suddenly the bomber's snout
Showed a blinking signal light.
"Looks as though she's ours, all right,"
Grunted Cole, "though who's to read
Signals flashed at such a speed?"
Cole had been the first to spring
To the bridge's narrow wing
Where he held a Lewis gun
On the shadow in the sun.

Closer—closer—overhead!
Not till then we saw the dread
Crosses on the underside
Of her wings.   "Let fly!" I cried,
But my voice was wholly drowned
In the hurricane of sound
As the Focke-Wulfe whipped past
'Thwartships—just above the mast—
Sound that in an instant froze
When a waterspout arose
Not a hundred yards abeam.
(This was like a crazy dream
Where all sound and motion ceased
'Till some trigger nerve released
Senses that the bomb had jammed.)
Bang!   A giant door was slammed
In my face.   *Bergetta* reared
As in pain—then vision cleared.

Tilted in an easy turn,
Now the plane swept well astern—
Straightened out—Cole harshly laughed,
"Going to try it fore and aft
Like she should have done at first.
Here's a chance for one good burst!"
This was not the Cole who moaned
Over debts and money loaned,
Not the man whose humour froze
Chilled by his domestic woes.
Framed within the questing ring
Of his sight came death a-wing,
Wicked, swift, completely real—
Something that could clink the steel
In his make-up, long unguessed.
For the moment he possessed
That for which we drab ones pray—
Courage that is sure and gay.

Now the bomber blazed her path
With a spitting gale of wrath.
Tracers slashed the sea, then ran
Fuse-like, where our wake began;
Reached *Bergetta*—ripped her deck—
Left the starboard boat a wreck.
Splintered concrete on the back
Of the armoured wireless shack.
Yet, through all the devil's din
As the great machine swooped in,
Low and steady for the kill,
Cole stood firm, his Lewis still,
Holding fire till he could trace
Details (like the pilot's face).

Then he opened up the gun,
Let the fiery hose-pipe run!
Harmless-looking wisps of smoke
All around the cockpit broke
And the bomber's brutal nose,
Quivered sharply, upward rose—
Rose, then dipped—We heard her scream
As she banked and dived abeam,
Blind, completely robbed of will,
With her motors roaring still—
Roaring till she hit the gray
Sea five cable-lengths away—
Hit and sudden disappeared
In an awful blast.   A weird
Sheet of water climbed the sky,
Swayed like washing out to dry,
Slowly dropped—and not a trace
Of the bomber marked the place.

Through the air exploded thin
Waves of silence shouldered in,
Silence that was so profound
It had impact sharp as sound.
Partly stunned, confused of mind,
Frantically I sought to find
What it was I'd heard destroyed
To create this ghastly void.
Then I knew!   Beneath my feet
There no longer was the beat
Of *Bergetta's* heart.   My own
Halted till the telephone
Brought the Chief's indignant shout,
"What the hell's it all about?"
"Nothing now," I said, "it's done."
"Must have been a proper one,"

Growled the Chief. "The filthy hound
Knocked my engine-room around.
Call you when I've learned the worst—
Better check it over first."

Ten long minutes, then the Chief
Came up top to air his grief.
"Several hours—engines stopped.
Feared it when the pressure dropped.
Never saw a little shake
Cause so many things to break.
Hardly like *Bergetta's* luck.
Lawks, we're just a sitting duck!"
"Make it fast," I urged. "No doubt
Jerry heard our call go out
When the ruddy plane attacked."
"If I dawdle, have me sacked,"
Burred the Chief, yet made scant haste,
Rubbed his hands on oily waste,
Clumped below decks with the grand
Manner only Chiefs command.
Not that I was left disturbed—
Fastest Chiefs are unperturbed.

God, the ocean's loneliness!
All the worse since one could guess
That no certain guarantee
Lay in that which eye could see.
Even now, beneath the gray
Waste a score of miles away
Hidden, hunting eyes might view
Easy prey. For once the blue
Cloudless sky brought no delight.
Fog or rain or blackest night
Would have been a glad relief.

Down below the sweating Chief
Drove his men who would, at length,
Give *Bergetta* back her strength—
Strength to fight, to dodge, to run.
Minutes crawled.   The very sun
Seemed to halt its westward swing
Just to watch our suffering.

Then the Chief, from down below,
Cried, "Two hours more to go."

Later, as the daylight waned,
Cole snatched up the glass and strained
Forward on the bridge's rail,
Focusing.   His face was pale
When he handed me the glass.
"If You will this cup should pass,
I'll be grateful, Lord," he said.
Then I saw it—far ahead
On the surface, low and lean
It had come—the submarine.

There was little left to do;
Through the day the four-inch crew
Had been mustered.   Books were stored
Ready to go overboard
In their weighted box.   Outswung
Lifeboats in their davits hung,
Stores and gear all lashed in place
For the baleful "just in case".
Calling up the Chief I said,
"Submarine awash ahead.
Range too great to reach it there,
Even if our gun would bear—
Which it won't.   I've sent our call

But there's no reply at all,
So we're on our own.   How long?"
Chief replied, "I hope I'm wrong
But I'd say another hour
Till we rouse a kick of power."
Eye to glass, Cole lowly urged
"Speed him up.   The Hun's submerged!"

"Chief," I said, "that sneaking shark
Has another hour till dark
For his hunting.   Half will do.
Pass the word for all your crew
To clear out.   No man of mine
Waits below the waterline
For this thing."   Snapped Chief, "Since when
Have you answered for *my* men?
If there is a chance to take,
That decision's ours to make."

Minutes later he returned
To the phone, "I've never learned
Masters are, of all men, wise.
Sorry.   I apologize.
Engine-room has now been cleared."
From below some men appeared
Men with sweat and oil a-drip.
Quietly "Abandon ship"
Stations claimed them.   Lord, how still
Was the sunset!   Men would thrill
To its beauty past the rim
Of horizon where no grim
Hunter used the gold and rose
Laneway as a screen to close.

Oh, how still!   The waiting men
Seldom spoke, and even then
Only murmured.   Soft, the swell
Whispered as it rose and fell.
Beauty walked the dusk—and death
While *Bergetta* held her breath.
Then, so clear, from down below
Came a ringing hammer blow—
And another—clink—clink—clink—
"Ah," said Cole, "I rather think
Chief's obedience has veered
Since the engine-room was cleared."

"Yes," I answered.   "By my check
Five have still to come on deck."
"Well?" jerked Cole.   I shook my head.
"It's their right to choose," I said.

Clink—clink—clink—.   The western glow
Turned to purple in the slow
Death of twilight.   Clink—clink—clink—
I could feel my innards shrink
Coldly as a wavelet's cream
Streaked the gloaming out abeam.
Still the sounding hammer smote
Down below; each steady note
Sang as it was coined and flung
Out where furtive silence clung.

Clink—clink—clink.   No warning came
With the "fish".   A spire of flame
Leaped.   A giant's frenzied grip
From the ocean snatched the ship;
Crushed it, tore it, hurled it back—
Mercifully the world went black.

PART XII

"You needn't go, of course," the Owner told me.
"She's no *Bergetta*—and it's yours to say.
The Yanks are digging up these 'Last War Babies'
And fitting them for sea down Houston way.
They're bottoms, though, and even if they're cranky
We'll sell our souls for anything that steers.
They call her *Sarah Clamp*.   I think they mentioned
She'd been laid up for nearly seven years."

"She's mine," I said.   I'd had enough of waiting
With memories.   The tear along my head
Was healed.   Young Cole was writing for his ticket,
And Bos' was back at sea, and Chief was dead.
The spell I'd had with Bessie down in Devon
Had soothed at first, yet ended in unrest
That had no answer.   When I'd talked of leaving
She'd said with unraised voice, "I think it's best."

The Owner growled, "Good man, I knew you'd do it!
Just shake her down and bring her to this side.
You'll have the time to make the single voyage
And still commission *Greta* on the Clyde."
He mentioned our new flagship that was building
Half casually, with humour in his eyes.
"She goes to you, of course—and save the effort
Of raising an expression of surprise."

Poor *Sarah Clamp*, she'd never been a beauty,
Not even when they'd launched her in 'Eighteen,
A mass-produced flush-decker out of Portland—
But now the idle years had left her green
And rather corpse-like.   Flocks of chipping hammers
Were pecking her like vultures on the day
When first I saw her—pecking till her carcass
Showed firm where rusted skin was chewed away.

Half fugitive, the breakers' yard had eyed her
As age and long disuse had taken toll,
And yet she had her own strange fascination
For anyone who sensed a vessel's soul.
Conceived in strife, with crisis in her rivets,
Grown old in peace that would not use her best,
Her cancelled youth returned to second waking
As England's peril gave existence zest.

Half-drudge, half-warhorse, snorting to a battle
Blown back on memory's wind across the years,
She flexed her stiffened joints beneath the urging
Of tough but friendly Gulf Port engineers,
And in her rousing strength I heard the whisper
Of something greater—from her very core
The heartbeat of Americans who'd built her
A generation past—to win a war.

Sound *Sarah*, there was nothing she was lacking
That steel and honest labour couldn't patch
But, as the fitters left her to my keeping,
I knew she had a crew that didn't match.
They'd lived ashore in lodgings while we'd waited,
A gang of trouble-makers from the first,
And now, with sailing date around the corner,
I really saw them—saw them at their worst.

I'd always worked with "Company" men. Their mothers
Had never marked them down as plaster saints.
They had their lusty faults—were rough and ready,
Well stocked with average sailormen's complaints.
Yet fine or foul, a single strain persisted
Beneath the outward show each man-jack made.
It came with him to every undertaking—
The common, decent instincts of his trade.

He often cursed his Company—but he claimed it.
He often damned his vessel, but *his* tongue
Held private rights; just let another blast her
And, in an instant, fists were being swung.
He learned his job like any other craftsman
And, since it made demands on him, set store
On holding it. So lived the Merchant Seaman
I'd known—and been—in years before the war.

How much I would have given for a dozen
Of such as these in days that were to come!
But *Sarah's* older men were mostly scrapings
And many of her younger hands were scum;
Old stiffs with records riddled by desertions,
The worst ones giving colour to the whole,
And, aping them, a landward lot of dodgers—
Young toughs who'd known no living but the dole.

As passengers they'd made the trip from England
And found the work on *Sarah Clamp* delayed.
Six weeks they'd lived ashore while waiting for her,
In good hotels, with all expenses paid,
And stiff advances—though they didn't need them
With Texan generosity so near.
What ho! the life of Merchant Navy heroes
Who dared the U-boats on a sea of beer!

Two days it took to finally collect them
When time arrived to move the crew aboard.
Dragged sullenly from jail, hotel and brothel,
They soldiered while the ship was fuelled and stored,
And, taking toll, a passion mounted in me,
A vow to get the *Sarah Clamp* away
At any cost—to slip the fouling fetters
Clamped on by smirking masters of delay.

The ship, I knew, remained a loafer's heaven
As long as she stayed handy to the beach,
And every move these vermin made was plotted
To keep that happy hunting-ground in reach.
The gauge unwatched that cost a week of waiting,
The careless sweat-rag clogging up a pipe,
The deck-gear smashed through throttles badly handled,
All stank of wharf-rats running true to type.

As long as patience lived I fought for reason.
I told them when I mustered them on deck,
"Remember, while this ship is kept from sailing
It's England, not the Company that you wreck.
Your wives, your kids are waiting for the cargo
And no one's here to get it home but you.
The fun's been had—let's see if you can earn it;
You've talked like men—let's see what you can do."

"Old stuff," one sneered.   "You press us on a hooker
That's half a hulk, and set us firing slag
The Yanks call coal—and when the profit's threatened
You put the blame on us—or wave the flag.
We're no one's slaves—" "You're damned sight worse,"
     I told him.
"You're traitors—gutless liars—every one."
"That moves no ship," he purred. "Perhaps a bonus—"
"Perhaps," I roared, "but first I'll use a gun."

I drove the ship to Norfolk—got her loaded,
Then pushed ahead towards Halifax at last.
I never used the gun—though I was tempted.
Each day was like a whip-stroke as it passed.
At times, I think, I half enjoyed the battle
That saw my scrounging devils come to heel.
I heard their jibes, I saw their filthy glances,
But these were blows I scarcely seemed to feel.

The punishment I took was in the watches
That found me nightly on the bridge alone,
When Chief returned and lusty, bull-voiced **Barney**
And scores of other seamen I had known;
When, once again, I found myself in London
With Derek—and again I saw the slow,
Apologetic smile he'd give his wrist-watch
Before he'd say, "Oh hang, I've got to go."

Here were the ones who'd died—or might be **dying**
Tonight to keep my mangy pack alive;
The lions and the eagles spent in winning
A chance for skulking jackals to survive.
What mattered if we won or lost—if winning,
We found our freedom gutted of all worth,
If brave men's dreams and lives were cancelled **coinage**
And spineless rogues inherited the earth?

Ugly and fearful things grow fat in darkness.
No sleepless mother ever viewed the dawn
More gratefully than I.   On every morning
The face I shaved was colourless and drawn
Till daylight threw a switch and left me fitted
To wring the grudging effort from my crew,
To clear the mists of still-uncertain evil
And face the certain evil that I knew.

And so we came to Halifax.   Old *Sarah*
Had happy quivers as we passed the gate,
But none there were for me—a British **Master**
Who'd brought his vessel in a full month late.
That afternoon I faced the tall Commander
Beneath whose touch each convoy took its **form**,
And told him how I'd failed—that I was sorry.
"Sit down," he said.   I waited for the storm.

But none blew up. He simply said, "*Bergetta*
Was quite a lady, and you're quite a man.
I've known no finer—and I've seen each vessel,
And every Captain here since war began.

"Since war began—" his thoughtful eyes were on me—
"How long since you have had a proper rest?"
"I've done all right," I said. "Perhaps," he countered,
"But look, we'll see a doctor—he'll know best."

"I tell you I'm all right," I cried, "There's nothing
To stop me taking *Sarah Clamp* across."
"Perhaps," he said again, "but let's make certain."
His firm insistence left me at a loss.
I knew I'd dropped some weight, that I was weary,
But that could all be righted in a week.
"I'm fine," I said—then stupidly discovered
That helpless tears were streaming down my cheek.

PART XIII

THIS was a tale for which to look
In some romantic story-book,
A dream to dream but not to take
To daylight and a world awake,
The sort of thing that came, perhaps,
With rare good luck to other chaps—
Yet here, for normal eye to see,
The miracle had come to me!

I woke at Fairlee! There had been
Two drab and hazy months between;
Long, pointless days, and horrid nights
When I had shouted for the lights.

Aye, even when I'd raised my head
One day—and Bess was by the bed—
The impact had no power to shake
That sense of being half-awake.

In fact, I really didn't care
What favouring wind had brought her there—
One thing I knew, and it required
No effort of a brain grown tired:
I knew that I was through.   No friend
Nor any man would now depend
On what I thought or felt or said
Or did in all the years ahead.

There's something that is faintly sweet
In sweeping and complete defeat
That ends a hopeless fight and brings
Release from torn, courageous things.
In twilight such as this I lay,
Content with each eventless day,
Content to feel the dead caress
Of listless, painless nothingness.

The days we travelled on the train
Weren't worth the trouble to explain.
Blue mountains surging from the sea
Pricked at my curiosity
The slightest bit, but fog banks closed
Their curtains, and again I dozed
Until one word like thunder broke—
Fairlee!   I trembled—and awoke.

Fairlee!   The smell of pines gave proof
I really lay beneath its roof
That first strange night.   Aye, Bess was there,
Wan-faced beside me in her chair,

To hear, to touch—but it was scent
Of Fairlee's trees that came and went
Like waves of consciousness until
The taunting voice of doubt was still.

Dear Lord, the wonder of the dawn
When silhouettes of leaves were drawn
Upon the glowing squares of wall!
Intent, I watched the clean light fall
On Bess, now nestled at my side;
It touched her lids—then, open-eyed,
She met my gaze and murmured low,
"It's true—oh, Jack—it's really so."

"Perhaps," I said, "you might make clear
Exactly how we've happened here."
"That's quickly done," my lass returned.
"The Owner phoned me when he learned
About your crack-up—had a berth
Reserved for me—said I was worth
A dozen doctors on the spot.
So out I came—and that's the lot."

"Not quite," I said. "You haven't told
What sort of magic spell you hold
On Fairlee's tenant—by what grace
We act as though we owned the place."
"The spell I hold," she laughed, "is this—"
And offered me her mouth to kiss—
"The place *is* ours, dear—yours and mine
Since August, Nineteen Thirty-Nine."

I gaped. "You did what I refused?"
"There was my money to be used,"
She answered. "Here is where it went.
Fairlee became my testament

Of faith. Are you about to say
That it was money thrown away?"
Her smile was flecked with shades of doubt
That vanished when my arms went out.

Oh, lovely Fairlee! Words are pale
Recorders of the wondrous tale
The next months wrote. No dream come true
Could match the happiness we knew
As, day by day, the healing touch
Of God in Nature broke the clutch
Despair had sunk on frame and mind,
And sight was granted to the blind.

Who loves the sea must love the earth
When it is raw with change and birth
And death that swells again to life.
Who once has seen a ploughshare knife
Through autumn turf and smelled the strength
Unloosed in every furrow's length,
Must find response in heart and nerve
Should he, in time, the ocean serve.

The forces that refreshed the soul
Ran deep and made my body whole,
Until no mountain trail could balk
The vigour of my daily walk.
New wisdom, too, when work was done,
Came to me through my neighbour's son
As, on our common beach, I'd hold
Discussion with the five-year-old.

The voices one could hear in shells,
The treasure-trove that little swells
Rolled on the ocean's hissing rim,
Were just an open book to him,

While I, poor fool, had all to learn.
What high adventure to return
To that sane world I hadn't known
Since I had been a child alone.

Yet cloud, no bigger than a hand,
Brushed the horizon of that land;
At first so faint, so far away,
It seemed that each succeeding day
Would find it gone.   Both Bess and I
Sternly ignored the patch of sky
It stained—but, all the time, we knew
The less we said the more it grew.

Not till the light began to slip
Away from our relationship
So swiftly that we felt the chill,
Had we the courage or the will
To face the truth—that soon I'd be
In shape again to go to sea;
That Fairlee could, at most, avail
A pause beside a bitter trail.

Rigid beside me in the night,
Bess forced the words, "You'd better write.
Tell them you're ready.   Make it fast—
Oh, it was wrong that it should last
As long as this—so long I've grown
To feel I've something of my own.
Darling, I cannot stand this drift—
Make it tomorrow—clean and swift!"

Sharing her pain, I lay there dumb,
Moved lips from which no words would come,
Reached out with arms that would not stir,
And felt my silence ravage her;

Beat with my fists the wall, unseen,
That once again moved in between
To thwart our meeting—felt a spate
Of anguish that was close to hate.

Next day I cabled, but our need
To get new bearings with all speed
Left those in England unimpressed.
The Owner answered, "I'd suggest
You take your time; make doubly sure
That Canada has worked its cure.
We'll call you when your turn comes 'round
So, carry on—you lucky hound!"

Just three weeks later came the strange,
Long envelope that was to change
The course so sharply.   Bessie read
The name upon the letterhead
And asked, "Aren't those the ones you claimed
The old-time press gangs were ashamed
To deal with?"   "More or less," I laughed.
"You'll never find more hungry craft.

"It's just such firms who keep alive
The pierhead jump because they drive
Their ill-paid, ill-berthed men to prey
Upon each other—but they pay
Rare dividends.   You'll find they choose
The hardest cases for their crews,
Who'll take what little they can earn
Because they've nowhere else to turn;

"Blacklisted shellbacks, green young fools
Who've broken from corrective schools;
Shady, old masters, bucko mates
Who've found themselves in nasty straits

But held their tickets by a thread
When better companies dropped them dead.
Pity the chap in such a mess—"
"What do they want of you?" asked Bess.

Puzzled at first, and half amused,
I chuckled, "I am scarcely used
To pressing offers to compete
For office in the Hungry Fleet.
Some joker's had his fun—".   I read
The letter through again, then said
With sudden rage, "By God, I've heard
Of nerve—they *mean* it, every word!"

Bluntly the bid was there to see:
"It's come to notice you will be
Available to soon return
To duty.   You'll be glad to learn
We have a berth—though you must wait
And do a trip or two as Mate
Before we are prepared to hand
You something as your own command."

"I'm not too proud to go in charge
Of any harbour garbage barge,"
I gritted, "but I draw the line
At working for a lot of swine.
Why should they think—?"   A sudden shaft
Of knowledge shook me fore and aft.
I found a chair, sat deathly still.
Bess cried, "What's happened?   Are you ill?"

I shook my head—smiled, "Not a bit.
I doubt if I will feel more fit
In all the days I have to go.
Bessie, my pigeon, do you know

What that thing means? The wolves have track
Of word I'm not expected back.
They think that they can get me cheap—
Figure I'm short on board and keep."

"But Owner?" Bessie cried. I jarred.
"It's not his fault. He'll find it hard
To drop me—but the word's about
The waterfront I've petered out.
I know the signs—oh, he'll be kind
And, if I were hard up, he'd find
A shore job for me. As it is
I need no charity of his.

"I'm free, Bess, free! No man can sneer
At you and me together here.
We've given all—we've offered more—
And now they've dropped us from the war!"

PART XIV

NEVER was man more thoroughly content
Than I—until the start of 'Forty-Two.
Vibrant each day arrived, and restful went
As evening deepened Fairlee's green to blue.
Now there were friends to share our open fire,
And family life we'd always been denied,
With every need so simple that desire
Could constantly be met and satisfied.

Constantly? No—but marvellously near.
Perhaps I had expected rather more
Than happens to a lover when the fear
Of parting goes. Perhaps I'd come ashore

A mite too late to capture at its noon
The dream whose heart was Bess—but men mature
And waste scant time in crying for the moon
If earth is good—and close at hand—and sure.

It helps when neighbours show you they are proud
To have you with them. Once they dragged me down
To spin my convoy doings to a crowd
Of Victory Loan campaigners in the town.
And as I stumbled through the yarn I knew
The memory of the last time I'd addressed
A meeting—*Sarah Clamp's* unholy crew,
Who hadn't been so kindly or impressed.

If old unrest was storing up beneath
The joy of living, I was not aware.
Pearl Harbour happened—only to bequeath
The comfort that the States would do their share.
The lovely Caribbean burst in flame
With losses that were terrible to face,
And everywhere you looked disaster came,
Except to Fairlee—spared by act of grace.

Here all was ordered peace, one's life was paced
By sun and rain and seasons that defied
The maddest men to change them. Dusk erased
The petty doubts swept in on daylight's tide.
I had not asked for this—I'd had no choice,
And who could blame a man who made the most
Of fate? What sin to quietly rejoice
That journey's end had been a friendly coast?

The great so often pivots on the small;
For me it was a note that came from Cole,
Who told me he'd his own command and all
Was going well, though Huns were taking toll

58

Along the eastern seaboard.   Had I heard
That Bos'n had been running in the Med
With cargoes bound for Malta?   There'd been word
His ship had copped it, and that Bos' was dead.

I mentioned it to Bessie as we lay
Inviting sleep that night.   She sighed, "I know
How much you liked him.   What, dear, did you say
His name was?"   "It was all so long ago
I don't remember," was my lame reply.
"Just Bos'—he joined *Bergetta* at the start.
Well, off to sleep, old girl—" but, by and by,
I spoke again, "That fellow had a heart—"

Bess made no answer—probably she slept—
But I was strangely wakeful and each thought
Came out in spoken fragments.   Hours crept.
I murmured, "He'd a mother and I ought
To write her, I suppose.   What *was* his name?
They used to go to church when time allowed—
I've seen them on a Sunday—she was lame—
Bombed out, I think—her face was sweet, and proud—

"You couldn't blame her.   Bos' was such a man
As any mother would have claimed with pride—
Or any Master.   It was Bos' who ran
Bergetta half the time—I only tried
To keep the pace he set.   He would have found
Some answer for the mess in *Sarah Clamp*—
Men somehow reached their peak with him around.
They'll not replace a fellow of his stamp—

"How calm he was—how rugged to the core—
How gentle in his way.   How cleanly straight—
There was no pilfering in *our* Bos'n's store—
No ship's gear smuggled past the dockyard gate.

59

He should have lived—we'll need the ones like him
To build a decent world around—oh God,
Why should You let this happen?   Why not trim
Hell's bunkers with the scrounger and the sod?

"Bos' was Your man; he lived the things You set
Such store by—though some scoffers called him proud
Because he held convictions—wouldn't let
Himself be bullied by the feckless crowd.
Freedom he surely claimed, yet only used
To bring his labour dignity and zest
Within the law—he never once abused
Authority—he asked, and gave, the best.

"This was the chap dictators had to crush
To get their sleep at nights—and now he's done—"
How deeply thoughts can sear you in the hush
Of early morning!   "He was only one,"
I argued.   "There are others—legions—still.
Integrity is common to the clan.
His spirit lives—"   My heart spoke, "That it will!
As discontent within another man."

PART XV

BESS read the signs too well for me to hide
My inner mind.   "I knew you would decide
To write again," she said.   "You can't conceal
A move like that.   It's possible I feel
The current's tug before you realize
Its strength yourself.   No secrets, dear, no lies
If these are numbered days we are to spend.
Let them be ours, in frankness, till they end."

Simple to say—impossible to live!
There was too much uncertainty to give
A chap a fighting chance.   Within the year
Owner had taken ill.   He couldn't hear
My fresh appeal to find a new command.
Strangers at court would never understand
The way he would have done—and yet the need
For senior Masters must be great indeed.

Hopelessness pressing hope, emotion's flood
Ruffled my mind's smooth channel, stirred the mud
Complacency had settled on its floor—
Until its swirling, clouded waters bore
Me blindly back to that insistent tide
Of ships by which my country lived or died,
The tide whose claim no Briton could avoid
With one fine instinct in him undestroyed.

Frankness with Bess when everything was blurred
Confusion in myself?   The little bird
That once had scorned our vessel and had flown
To overtake its comrades, had not known
An ordered plan.   It must have felt the grip
Of certainty and safety that the ship
Had offered; yet a single fear it knew—
Of being denied the trail its fellows flew.

Lucky that bird, for it was mine to say
If it should have its chance, if it should stay—
No one, when my turn came, would understand
And spring the cage's door with friendly hand.

* * *

High on the slope, with Fairlee at my feet,
Had come the rally in my blind retreat.
The bitterness the firm's reply had spilled

Ran thin and, as it dwindled, I was filled
With melancholy calm—a gift to those
Who know they've reached the climax of their woes.
"Somewhere the track leads on," I thought, "but where?
God in Your heaven, tell me—if You're there."

"I have no will to do but what is right
Yet here I am, rejected, in a fight
I never feared and, gladly, still would own.
Fairlee is haunted ground that Bos' has sown
With discontent I cannot understand.
Now in the quiet of the world I planned
There is no peace—and yet the world outside
Brings nothing but the flogging of my pride.

"Truly I'd serve—I'm not afraid to die.
I know that if we fail, the men who lie
With good, clean sea above them will alone
Be envied—but the choice is not my own."

What was that echo?   Was it Bos'n's voice?
"The ruddy fool *believes* he has no choice!"

Silence was on the mountains and the sea.
Along the beach the mist was drifting free
And, in the woods, the rain's accented drip
Grew slower, slower.   From the Gulf a ship
Spoke hoarsely as it felt its cautious way
Through fog that still hung low beyond the bay;
Some hard, old tramp, I wagered, from her tone—
A bellow, half defiant, half a groan.

What was it Peter Dalsbo once had said?
"The voyage pays, whatever lies ahead,
As long as I have given all I'm worth."
Where was he now?   No doubt he'd found a berth

Despite his crippled hands.   The sea had need
Of one who could perpetuate *his* breed.
"Faith leaps from life to life," had been his claim,
"Until, one day, you find from whence it came."

Had it been faith that Bos' had passed to me;
The anguish that no longer left me free
To cherish Fairlee?   Faith was something strong
And comforting that helped a man along—
Along to what?   Unchallenging content?
Faith had been there when Bess's father spent
His last, hard night not far from Jordan's stream,
And yet he died next morning, with his dream.

Out on the Gulf the fog had risen now.
Half conciously I watched the freighter plough
Abreast the bay, and marked the white and blue
Of Greece's vivid ensign that she flew;
One spot of colour on a bleak array
Of ship and deck-load painted dirty gray—
So like the Greeks themselves, whom exile failed
To cow—whose flashing spirit never paled.

A hard ship this—aye, even for a Greek.
Plain, British-built, her type had known its peak
Around the period of Nineteen-Ten.
She'd have live sheep in some ill-smelling pen
Beneath the whaleback—for the Greeks have proof
That meat keeps fresh much cheaper on the hoof.
And there'd be whiffs of garlic down below,
And pictures of the Greece of long ago.

Pictures of ancient Athens on its hill
And Mount Olympus where guerrillas still
Drew bead with eyes whose freeman's passion fed
On storied past—and misted hope ahead.

Glory there was in that old craft as she,
Resolute, put her shoulder to the sea—
Glory in dirt and squalor of a tramp?
Had there been glory in the *Sarah Clamp*?

Had there been aught among that weasel crew
Worth saving from the old world for the new
If we should hold our freedom, win the right
To mould the new?   The only mark of fight
They'd shown had been to savagely defend
Their sloppy self-indulgence to the end,
Their thirst for beer and victuals, labour-free—
A thirst as great as Fairlee was for me!

Fairlee and spineless loafers in one breath?
Nonsense!   I'd faced my share of salted death
For England; I'd claimed naught but what I'd earned
By sweat and loneliness and lessons learned
The hard way.   What I asked was clean and good.
I blocked no other's living space—I stood
Absolved of blame for any running sore
That sapped the nation's strength for making war.

Talk to the grasping Owner who had seen
The seamen as a cog in his machine,
Talk to the crooked union delegate
Who filled his pockets teaching men to hate,
Talk to the fattened landlord of the slum
From which the dole-bred wolves—and I—had come,
Talk to the politician who could speak
One thing and do another, tongue in cheek—
Talk to them all, demand that they atone,
But leave an honest sailorman alone!

Plugging along, the tramp was not impressed.
It altered course a little to the West

And rolled some greasy smoke across its stern.
"Sorry," it seemed to say, "that's your concern.
I've far to go and pressing work to do."
Wryly I took the rebuff, for I knew
I'd desperately been laying down a screen
To fog an issue all too clearly seen.

Somewhere the track led on—if I'd be led.
The Hungry Fleet was there; the note had said
To take my time—they'd be prepared to wait—
It wasn't difficult to place a Mate.
Here, if my pride could stand it, I might find
At least a temporary peace of mind
Till death stepped in or victory should bring
Me back to Fairlee for a second spring.

Face it, accept it—history didn't care
How stupid was my firm, how damned unfair.
It would record that certain convoys sailed
Or faltered when the flow of seamen failed;
That some one nation's people learned to serve
At any post they could and didn't swerve
Until the day was won; that private woes
When nursed had proven deadliest of foes.

Well, I'd go back—'twas only common sense.
I had to—or go mad with the suspense.
God alone knew how long I could survive
A hungry ship, ill-fitted and alive
With cheating stewards, sailors well aware
Of all the dismal past that brought me there—
"D'you ever hear of *Sarah Clamp*? That's him!"
Oh, but they'd slowly tear me limb from limb.

Sunset was close. The first of evening's chill
Edged the remoteness of the sea and hill,

Heightened the utter loneliness that drained
Blood from my heart and left a void that pained.
Nothing I'd ever known had been as bleak;
Blind fog that once had held me for a week
With icy, breaking reefs on either beam
Had been, compared to this, a clouded dream.

Dalsbo, his dead about him, must have known
Something like this when facing night alone
Hunched in his lifeboat.   Bessie, at the start,
Left to herself, my child beneath her heart,
Had savoured desolation.   Even Bos'
To whom great power always had been close,
Must have been wracked before he learned to stand
Unflinching, with no other soul at hand.

There had been Bess's father, too, who'd seen
Visions of reborn England, tough and clean.
He'd been alone—Gethsemane hard by—
Maybe he'd been there!   Could it be that I
Was in their footsteps, drawing near the source
From which had come their certainty and force,
Their quiet patience?   What had Bessie found?
Ah yes, "a really honest battleground".

Not just a home to save, a man to hold,
But something greater—infinitely bold,
An outpost of a land from which would rise
Men with a clearer purpose in their eyes.
Rueful amusement was the most she'd raised
In me, although her gentle faith had blazed
Through ugly years—the only thing that warmed
Existence I'd found stunted and deformed.

Was it she'd seen what prophets first must see
Who bring their people vision?   Men like me

Would sail to hell with one who came along
Sparing no weakness, someone who was strong
And human and who asked for no reward
Except a full offensive with the Lord
Plotting the course; a man who could release
Strength for the war, reality for peace.

One of God's men with fire enough to raise
The act beyond the level of the phrase!
I saw him clearly, fearless in the truth
That wins the quick, hard loyalty of youth;
Stirring the sluggard till he could achieve
A prize to fight for, something to believe,
Rousing a patriotism more than blind
Defensive will—aggressiveness of mind.

Easy, belay! Just what had this to do
With one who faced a crumby ship—a crew
To whom the pious word was bilge? They'd gang
A saint and break his heart without a pang.
Easy, belay! And yet, why not? A scamp
Was still a man. Aboard the *Sarah Clamp*
There'd been one lack—a fighter who had pride
And yet could cast his arrogance aside.

Someone who'd known despair and want and lies
Yet hadn't let their seepage crystallize;
In whose clear mind the key to freedom lay
For all, since selfish ends were cast away
And common weal become his one concern.
This was an office he could never learn
From books. It had to happen—through a Touch—
Because he wanted nothing else so much.

There was excitement in me. Far below
Fairlee lay gilded in the afterglow—

Lovely beyond all words.   My eye passed on,
Out where the grimy tramp from Greece had gone
Riding the sunset down.   Perhaps that track
Even in peace would see no coming back.
There was scant use, I knew, to make a start
Carrying limitations in my heart.

That was the point; the man who set his feet
Defensively had but one move—retreat.
Humbly I faced the ocean, well aware
Of trial by fire that waited for me there.
Facing the worst, yet ready for its wrack—
This was *my* tune to call.   It was "Attack!"
Not as a desperate thrust at the unknown;
There was a plan—I wouldn't sail alone.

Lighted, the windows of the living-room
At Fairlee smouldered softly in the gloom
Cast by the oak trees.   There'd be much to say
To Bess; the leaden words that yesterday
Had lacked all ring were eager now and bright.
Love would be there beneath the eaves tonight,
Complete, with endless power to endure.
I knew it from that moment, knew for sure.

Then, as I started down the trail I heard
A voice say, "Wait!"—a gently spoken word
That brought my head up.   Far across the blue
Of dusk the peak of Baker thrust in view,
Mighty, serene—held firmly in one ray
Which still escaped the passing of the day.
The cage stood wide—strong-winged my spirit rose
And met God's smile upon the soaring snows.